"Tiger Watch" at Pebble Beach during the 2000 U.S. Open.

1

Publisher: Spurlock Photography, Inc.
Managing/Photo Editor: Brian Spurlock, Spurlock Photography, Inc.
Editor: Jai Giffin, Host Communications, Inc.
Design: Bob Slater, Kim Troxall, Host Communications, Inc.
Editorial Assistance: Mark Buerger, Host Communications, Inc.
Photographers: Corbis, Inc., David Strick/Corbis Outline, Jay Crihfield, Tom DiPace, Richard Dole, David Gonzales, Icon Sports Media (Robert Beck, John Biever, Jim Gund, Larry Lambrecht), SIPA Press (Jeff Christensen, Rose Prouser, Ammar ABD Rabbo), Sportschrome (Bongarts, Sport The Library, Rob Tringali, Michael Zito), and Brian Spurlock.
Production: Host Communications, Inc. • 904 North Broadway • Lexington, KY 40505 (859) 226-4510

Front Cover Photos: Brian Spurlock
Front Cover Design: Kim Troxall, Host Communications, Inc.
Back Cover Photos: Brian Spurlock
Back Cover Design: Robert Silvers/Runaway Technology

Orders for this publication can be made by contacting:
Spurlock Photography, Inc.
P.O. Box 406
Fishers, Indiana 46038-0406
Phone: (317) 841-2857
Fax: (317) 841-2868

The cover price is $14.99 (Indiana residents add 5% sales tax). Payment can be made by money order, cashier's check, VISA or Mastercard.

TIGER'S WORLD

Tom Lehman, the 1996 PGA player of the year, stated, "The future of golf is Tiger Woods." At age 25, Tiger is the youngest golfer to win the career grand slam and hold all four major titles at once. Tiger Woods is in the process of rewriting the history book on golf, and a more appropriate statement now is that Tiger is the past, present and future of golf. His wins in the majors have come in impressive style. He won the 2000 U.S. Open at Pebble Beach by 15 strokes, which was the largest margin of victory in 100 years of the tournament. Tiger's 19-under-par effort at St. Andrews was the low-est score, in relation to par, in 140 years of the British Open. Tiger has already earned more than $25 million, placing him atop the career money list. At age 21, Tiger was the youngest player to be ranked the No. 1 golfer in the world. He is unquestionably the best golfer in this era and is in pursuit of Jack Nicklaus's record of 18 major wins.

Jack Nicklaus and Arnold Palmer, two of golf's greatest ambassadors, raised the bar of excellence for decades. Palmer, at the 1962 World Series of Golf said, "Jack Nicklaus is just a youngster and a newcomer to the pro-fessional ranks. But you gentlemen saw one

© All photos in section by Brian Spurlock

of the greatest out there today. He'll be a headliner for a long time and could put together the greatest career the game has ever known. He has everything."

Bobby Jones said after Jack shot a record 271 to win the 1965 Masters, "Jack Nicklaus plays a game with which I am not familiar."

The same types of statements made about Jack Nicklaus are being made today about Tiger Woods. Jack Nicklaus on Tiger Woods "… as talented a golfer as I have ever seen … Arnold Palmer and I agree that you could take his Masters and my Masters and add them together, and this kid should win more than that."

It seems only fitting as Jack Nicklaus was finishing the 18th green at Pebble Beach after 44 consecutive U.S. Opens that Tiger was getting ready to tee off on hole one. Jack Nicklaus played 17 years before his first winless season on the PGA tour and finished with 71 tour victories. Even more fitting was that Jack and Tiger were paired together in Jack's final PGA Championship. Photos of Tiger and Jack appear on pages 110-123.

I poured through thousands of Tiger Woods photos in putting this book together. There are more than 220 photos capturing the strength, grace, emotion, triumph and charm of golf's newest hero. Tiger is a great subject to photograph as he wears his emotions on his shirt sleeves. His repertoire of shots, and his ability to play a unique shot in difficult circumstances, is amazing. In the 2001 Advil Western Open, Tiger twice drove in the trees on the ninth hole, which is a 568-yard par-5 with a tight tree-lined fair-

way. On Thursday, as shown in the photo, he was about 30 yards behind a series of three trees with a small opening between them. Tiger took out an iron and hit it through the gap in the trees which was like threading a needle. Three days later, Tiger hit it in the same area again, except he was another 20 yards back, making a repeat shot almost impossible. I knelt down even with the trees and next to the gallery. There was about a 10-foot opening between the trees and myself. Everybody was thinking he would either punch out or slice the ball around the trees and back into the fairway. Instead he drills his second shot, which stayed about three feet above the ground and barely missed my head by a foot, and it lands 250 yards away pin high in a green side bunker. The amazing things are that he has pinpoint accu-

racy with an iron from the rough and that he hit the ball as far as he did with it staying so low to the ground. These two shots illustrate the enormous talent he has to pull those kinds of shots off.

Tiger also has a magical quality about him that isn't related to his golf swing. This is a true story that happened to a golfer from Canada who was on vacation at Pebble Beach and was having a hard time finding an open tee time. The golfer showed up several mornings in a row putting his name on a waiting list in case someone didn't show up for their tee time. After several days of no luck, the starter said that he had one tee time open with a threesome, but he would have to check with them to see if they wanted a fourth person in the group. The threesome said 'yes,' but the catch was that the threesome also paid for the time slot behind them so they wouldn't be rushed and no one would be behind them. The green fees are already about $300 a round which meant paying nearly $600 to play. The golfer figured this was going to be

his only chance in a lifetime to play Pebble Beach, so he agreed to pay the double green fee. To his amazement when he showed up at the first tee, he found out that he would be playing with Michael Jordan, Kevin Costner and Tiger Woods. Needless to say, it was the experience of a lifetime. When it was all over, Jordan, Costner and Woods paid for his round of golf and took him to dinner. Fairy tales do come true.

• • •

The back cover of the book is a photomosaic — a method of arranging hundreds of tiny photographs that when viewed from a distance, combine to form a single larger image. The photos on the back cover were taken by myself, but the final design was done by Robert Silvers of Runaway Technology. Robert has this process patented, and first created photomosaics as a class project while at the MIT media lab. Robert designed the software to consider not only the color and density of the photos or tiles

but also the shape of the objects within the tile. The computer software selection takes him so far, and then there is a lot of handwork involved to come up with the finished design. In this case hundreds of Tiger Woods photos were used to form a larger photo of Tiger Woods. Robert has been commissioned to do photomosaics of Bill Gates, Al Gore, and Jack Nicklaus. He was also hired by *Life* magazine to design the award-winning cover of their 60th Anniversary issue.

I hope that you enjoy not only the Photomosaic on the back cover, but all the photos in this book that help you see inside Tiger's World. Special thanks to everyone at Host Communications for their time and effort in putting this publication together. Special thanks to my attorney and father, Ben Spurlock, for his help in handling legal matters and contracts. Last, but not least, special thanks to my wife, Sally, for her support and love in putting this publication together.

$13.99

$14.99

Jeff Gordon book to be
released in late fall 2001

Prices include shipping and handling. Orders
can be obtained by contacting:

Spurlock Photography, Inc.
P.O. Box 406
Fishers, Indiana 46038-0406
Phone: (317) 841-2857
Fax: (317) 841-2868

THE
WONDER
YEARS

At age three, Tiger shot 48 for nine holes ... at age four-and-a-half, he recorded his first birdie ...
at age five, Tiger showed off his swing for Fran Tarkenton on "That's Incredible" ...

at age six, Tiger made his first hole-in-one ... by age eight, Woods shot in the 70s and beat his father for the first time over 18 holes. Tiger, at age 14 (shown above), had already recorded five holes-in-one and was featured in Sports Illustrated's *"Faces in the Crowd."*

Tiger and his father Earl Woods celebrate the 1991 USGA Junior Amateur Championship in Bay Hill, Fla. He later went on to claim the Junior Amateur Championship again in 1992 and 1993.

© Richard Dole

At age 16, Tiger played in the Los Angeles Open making him the youngest player ever to compete in a PGA event.

© Richard Dole

© Sportschrome USA

15

Eldrick Woods was given the nickname "Tiger" by his father to honor combat friend Nguyen Phong who saved Earl Woods' life during the Vietnam War.

© Richard Dole

© Robert Beck/Icon Sports

© Sportschrome USA

While at Stanford, Tiger won the 1996 NCAA Championship and was named College Player of the Year.

In 1994, 1995 and 1996, Woods won the U.S. Amateur Championship, joining Jack Nicklaus and Phil Mickelson as the only three golfers to win the NCAA and U.S. Amateur titles in the same year.

Top Left © David Gonzales; ©Richard Dole (2)

Tiger warms-up for the 2001 U.S. Open at Southern Hills with long-time coach Claude "Butch" Harmon looking on.

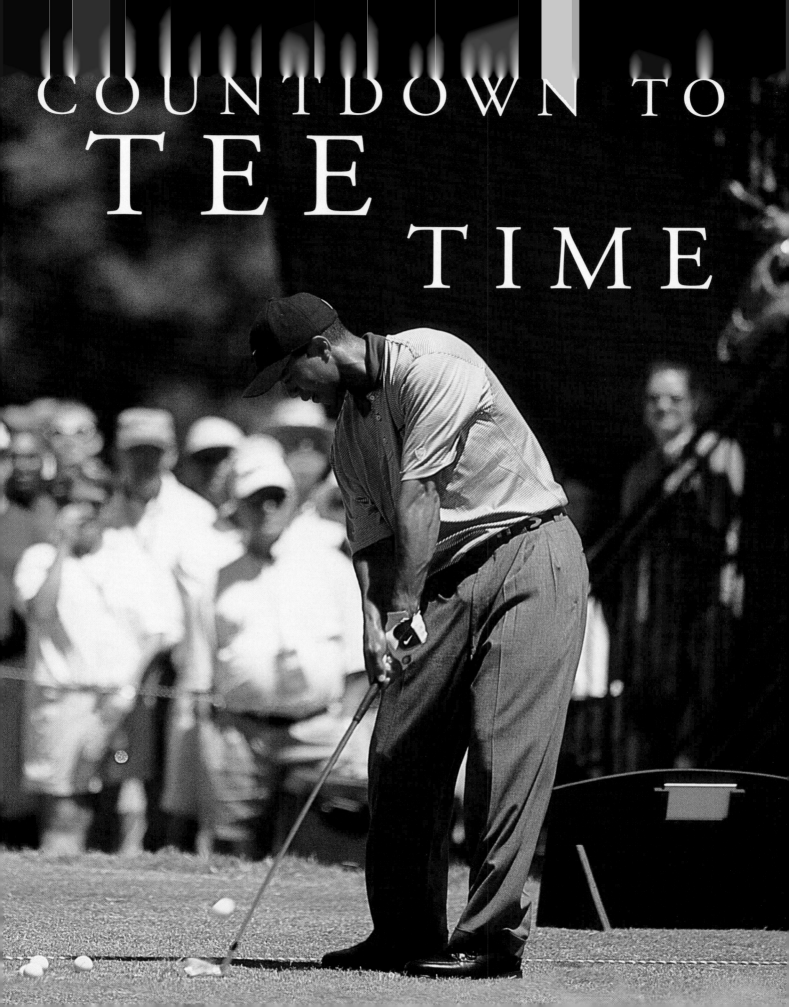

COUNTDOWN TO
TEE
TIME

Tiger shows up for work driving his courtesy Buick Regal. Caddy Steve Williams meets Tiger in the clubhouse parking lot 90 minutes before tee time.

TIGER WOODS

21

Tiger tuning up on the range at the 2001 U.S. Open in Tulsa, Oklahoma.

What's in Tiger's Bag?
- *Titleist Titanium 975D Driver*
- *Titleist Forged Prototype 2-9 Irons with True Temper Dynamic Gold Shafts*
- *Titleist Forged Prototype Pitching Wedge*
- *Titleist Vokey Design Sand Wedge and Lob Wedge*
- *Scotty Cameron By Titleist Pro Platinum Putter*

WOODS

TIGER WOODS

Tiger fuels up with an energy bar before the round begins.

© 2001 All Photos by Brian Spurlock

Tiger's signature head cover bears the inscription "Love From Mom," stitched by his mother in her native Thai.

USGA

Tiger
Woods

This high-motorized sequence at 10 frames per second captures Tiger's swing at approximately 123 mph. The ball blasts off the tee at more than 180 mph.

© 2001 Brian Spurlock

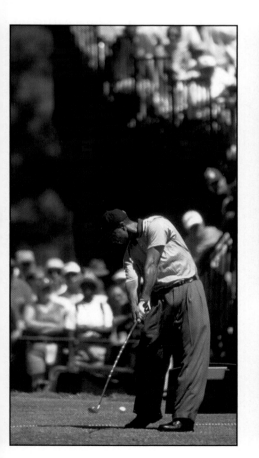

CLASSIC
TIGER

"*Grip it,*
and Rip it"

Tiger ponders his next shot while waiting in the fairway.

Tiger at the famous 18th tee at Pebble Beach.

On the 8th fairway at Pebble Beach, Tiger successfully completes his second shot across the ocean. This is considered by many golf enthusiasts as the most spectacular second shot in golf.

Tiger and his mother Kultida celebrate his 1997 win at the Motorola Western Open in Chicago.

Earl Woods on his son Tiger: "no fear of failure ... no fear of success ... none."

© 1997 Jay Crihfield/Spurlock Photography

© David Strick/Corbis Outline

At the 2000 British Open, Woods made history by becoming the youngest man to win the career grand slam with a 19-under 269 at St. Andrews. This was the lowest score in relation to par in the 140 years that major championships have been played.

Tiger's shot accuracy is arguably the best in the game. While taping his Nike commercial where he breaks out the windows, Tiger used a 5-iron in the first take and broke two of the three windows. During the remaining two takes, he was a perfect six-of-six, hitting every window he attempted.

© 2001 Brian Spurlock

Tiger in motion at the

2001 Advil Western Open.

Hitting out of the sand at the 1999 Phoenix Open.

Tiger blasts out of the sand en route to his first win at The Memorial in 1999.

Tiger, after using a wood from the fringe of the green, reacts after the ball barely misses the cup.

© 2001 Brian Spurlock

Tiger "raises the roof" at the Nissan Open.

At the 83rd PGA Championship, Tiger plays the 18th hole at the Atlanta Athletic Club. Tiger reacts to almost making a birdie at the 490-yard Par-4 over the water. Although not successful in winning his third straight PGA Championship, Tiger did return to his winning ways the following week by defeating Jim Furyk in a seven hole playoff to win his third straight WGC-NEC Invitational in Akron, Ohio.

At age 25, Tiger Woods is already the leading all-time career money winner with more than $25 million in earnings. Tiger has made more than 70 consecutive cuts, as well as 22 majors in a row.

Tiger Roars

One of the most photographed people in the world, Tiger Woods, plays the No. 7, par-3 hole at Pebble Beach, which is one of the most photographed golf holes in the world.

Ernie Els looks on as Tiger hits his approach shot from the scenic 9th fairway at Pebble Beach.

© 2000 Brian Spurlock

There were 11 Nike logos visible on Tiger's apparel on his first day of play as a professional.

© 2001 Brian Spurlock

Tiger reacts to his putt at the 2000 PGA Tournament at Valhalla.

Tiger celebrates with his patented fist pump as his caddy Steve Williams gets into the act.

In one of the greatest finishes in PGA history, Tiger sinks the "clutch" putt on the 18th green to force a playoff with Bob May.

© 2000 Brian Spurlock

Woods always wears the color red on Sunday because his mother feels that it's a lucky and "power color" for him.

© Michael Zito/Sportschrome USA

Johnnie Walker
Classic

*Tiger shows off his trophy after
winning the 1998 Johnnie Walker
Classic in his mother's native
Thailand.*

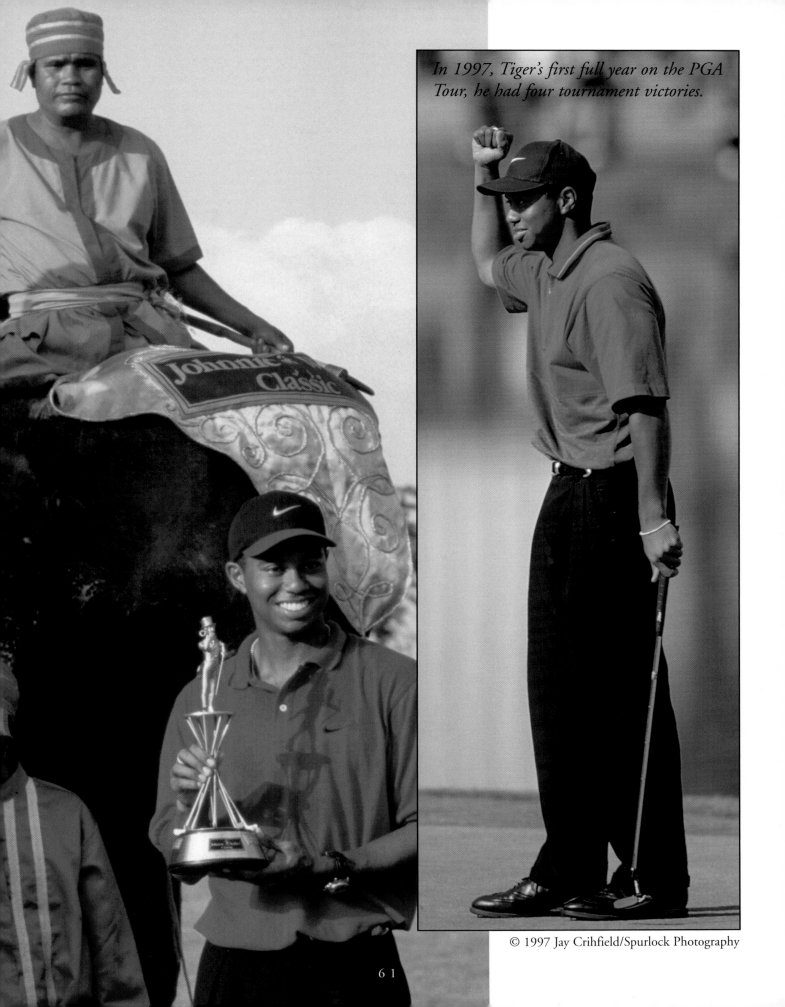

In 1997, Tiger's first full year on the PGA Tour, he had four tournament victories.

© 1997 Jay Crihfield/Spurlock Photography

At the 1999 Masters, fans gather to marvel at another one of Tiger's 300-plus yard drives.

© 2000 Brian Spurlock

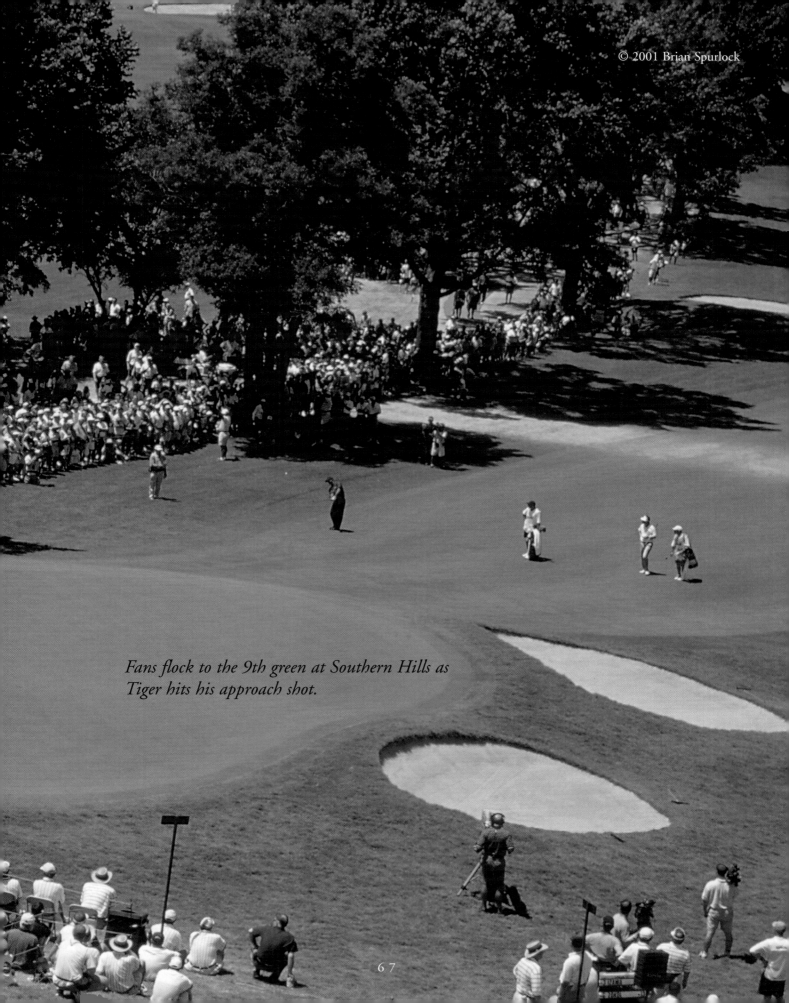

Fans flock to the 9th green at Southern Hills as Tiger hits his approach shot.

© 2001 Brian Spurlock

Tiger acknowledges the gallery on the 18th green just before clinching his third consecutive Memorial win.

Caddy Steve Williams and Tiger Woods celebrate a 15-stroke victory at the 2000 U.S. Open. This was the largest winning margin in 100 years of the event.

© 2000 Brian Spurlock

"It doesn't get any better than this ... to come here and perform the way I did on one of the greatest venues there is in golf ... You don't really understand what you've done until time passes."
— Tiger Woods on his win at the 2000 U.S. Open at Pebble Beach

© 2000 Brian Spurlock

© Rob Tringali Jr./Sportschrome USA

In 2000, Woods won the U.S. Open, British Open and the PGA Championship, becoming the first player since Ben Hogan in 1953 to win three majors in a year.

© 2000 Brian Spurlock

Tiger with his mom, Kultida, after his 2000 U.S. Open victory stated "the U.S. Open is the ultimate championship. At each level, the USGA has always been the top whether it's age division, amateur ranks or now in the pros. Winning your nation's title is very special."

© 2000 Brian Spurlock

Tiger holds or shares the record in relation to par in all four major championships. Sometimes his play is so dominant that his victories seem as easy as a "walk in the park."

YOU DA MAN

Tiger Woods shows he truly is "Da Man," reaching the green in two mighty swings on the 642-yard, par-5, fifth hole at Southern Hills. It is the longest hole in U.S. Open history. Even the official U.S. Open Press Kit said, "It's unlikely anyone will reach this green in two."

THE
19th
GREEN

Tiger arrives in his jet in Hamburg, Germany, to play in the Deutsche Bank/SAP Open.

*Tiger Woods at Nellis Air
Force Base in Las Vegas.*

© 1997 SIPA Press

At the All-Star Cafe Celebrity Sports Auction in New York City, Ken Griffey, Jr., Whoopi Goldberg and Tiger raise money to benefit Special Olympics International. © 1996 Jeff Christensen/SIPA Press

Larry King got Tiger Woods to sit down for his first lengthy live television interview.

Dubai Crown Prince Sheikh Mohammed Bin Rashed Al Maktoum gives Tiger a tour of his Go Dolphin Racing Stables.

Tiger visits with the horse "Dubai Tiger."

The blonde Tiger has more fun on the sidelines at the 2001 FedEx Orange Bowl with Alex Rodriguez.

Tiger cheers on his favorite team, the Los Angeles Lakers, from the front row at The Forum.

© 2001 Tom DiPace

© 1997 Michael Zito/Sportschrome USA

Two of the world's most famous athletes Muhammad Ali and Tiger Woods, together at Sports Illustrated's *celebration of the greatest athletes of the 20th century.*

Even celebrities like Bill Cosby (above) and Mickey Mouse present Tiger with awards, while in Thailand he received an honorary doctorate degree.

THE
GALLERY

The 18th green at Augusta.

© Brian Spurlock (5); Jim Biever/Icon Sports Media (2 - top right)

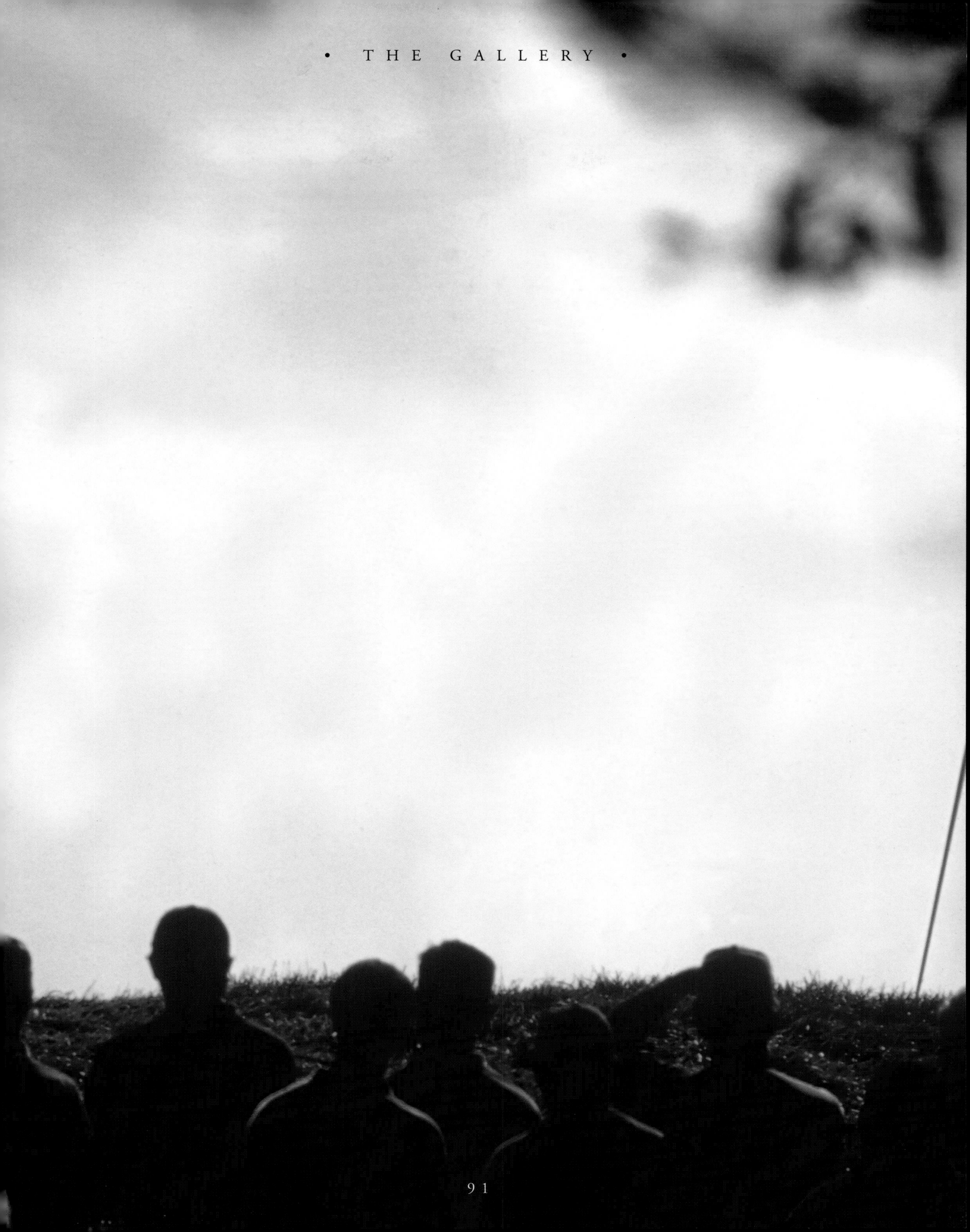

© Brian Spurlock (6); Jay Crihfield/Spurlock Photography (top middle); Ric Fogel/Sportfolio (1 - top right)

FACES
OF A
CHAMPION

© Brian Spurlock (3); Bongarts/Sportschrome USA (1 - top left)

© Jay Crihfield/Spurlock Photography (bottom left); All Other Photos Brian Spurlock

© All Photos by Brian Spurlock

© Brian Spurlock (4); Jay Crihfield/Spurlock Photography (bottom left)

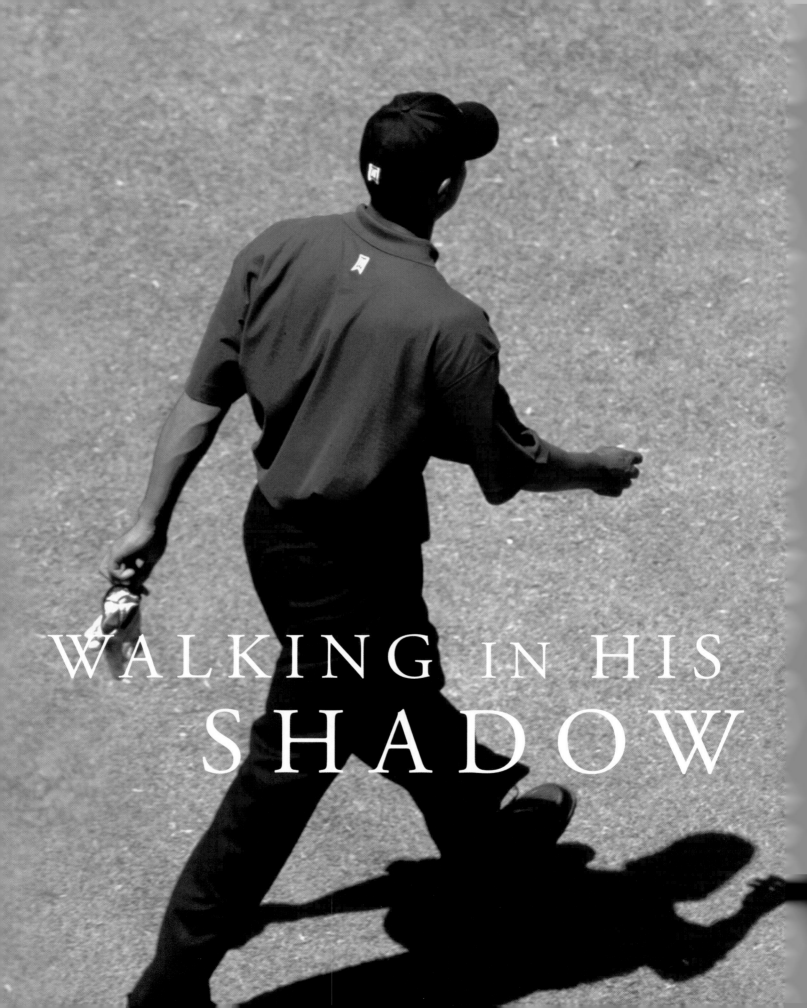

WALKING IN HIS SHADOW

Sergio Garcia, known as "El Niño," made his PGA European debut at age 15.

© 2000 Brian Spurlock

Sergio finished second and runner-up to Tiger in the 1999 PGA Championship. These two players are destined to square off in championship battles for many years to come on the PGA Tour.

© 1999 Brian Spurlock

Vijay Singh — winner of the 1998 PGA Championship and the 2000 Masters.

Ernie Els — a two-time U.S. Open Champion in 1994 and 1997.

© 2001 Brian Spurlock

© 2001 Brian Spurlock

Phil Mickelson began playing golf at the age of one-and-a-half. He won the 1989 and 1990 NCAA Championships and the 1990 U.S. Amateur. By age 26, Mickelson had won 10 tour events. Only Jack Nicklaus, Tiger Woods, Gene Sarazen and Horton Smith accomplished this feat at a younger age.

Davis Love III won the PGA Championship at Winged Foot in 1997.

© 2000 Brian Spurlock

David Duval won the 2001 British Open. The photos here are from the 2001 PGA Championship in Atlanta where Duval and Woods were paired together the first two days.

TIGER
& JACK

Jack Nicklaus hits his second shot from the scenic 9th fairway at Pebble Beach in his final U.S. Open. The Golden Bear won four U.S Opens (1962, 1967, 1972 and 1980).

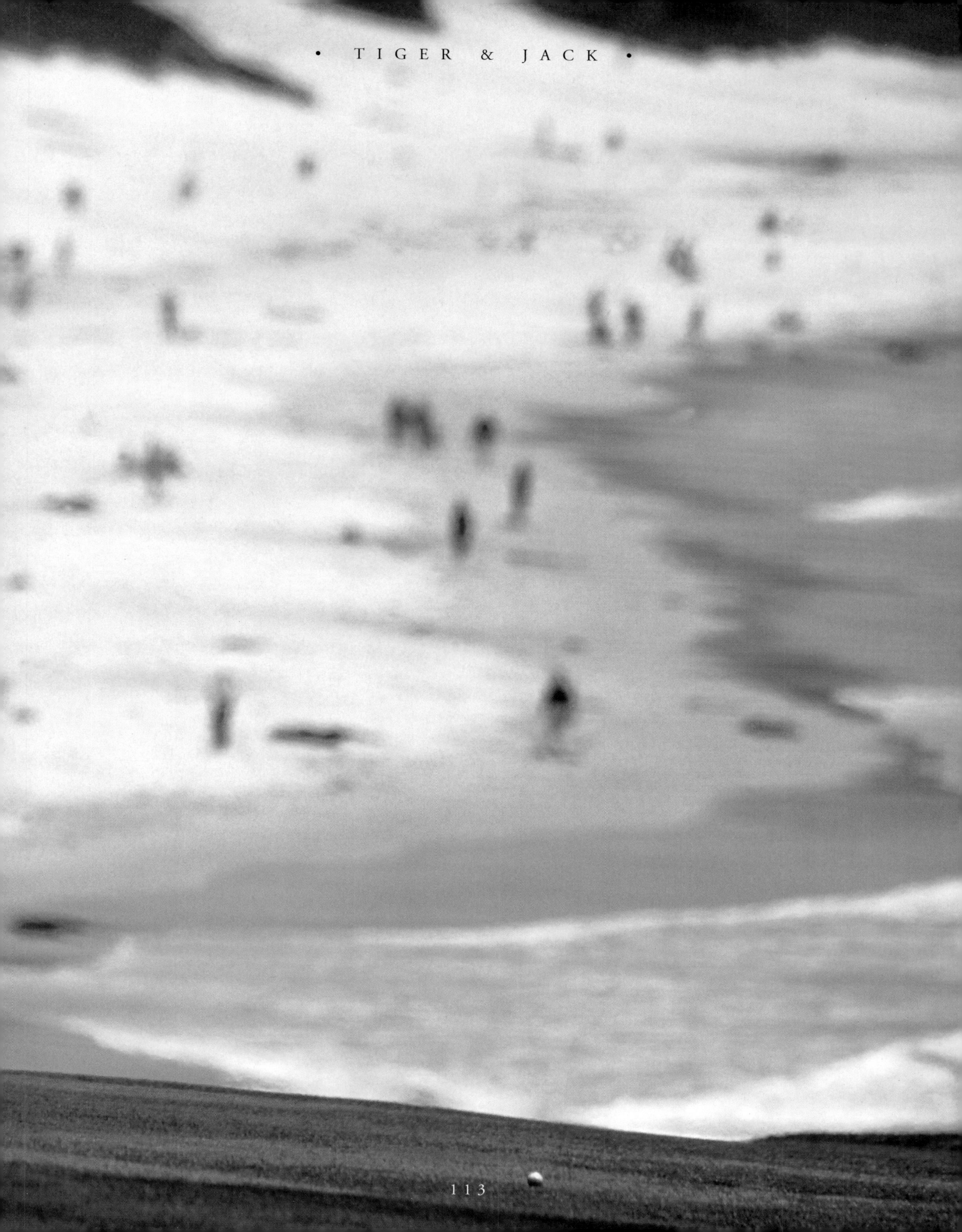

Tiger looks on as Nicklaus plays in his final PGA Championship at Valhalla in Louisville, Kentucky.

© 2000 Brian Spurlock

Nicklaus presents Tiger with his third consecutive trophy in The Memorial.

Paired with Jack Nicklaus, Tiger went on to win the 2000 PGA Championship. This was Woods' fifth major win as he pursues the record of 18 major championships held by Nicklaus.

Two of the greatest golfers of all time share a moment together.

© 2000 Brian Spurlock

*Jack gives Tiger a few tips before
teeing off on the first hole.*

Jack Nicklaus tees off at the 18th hole at Pebble Beach in the 1992 U.S. Open.

HOLE 18
YARDS 543
PAR 5

At the 18th hole at Pebble Beach, Jack Nicklaus reflects on memories from 44 consecutive U.S. Opens. This would be his final hole in U.S. Open competition.

THE TROPHY
COLLECTION

© John Biever/Icon Sports Media

© (from top left to right) Rob Tringali/Sportschrome USA; Robert Beck/Icon Sports Media;
Jay Crihfield/Spurlock Photography; Larry Lambrecht/Icon Sports Media; Brian Spurlock

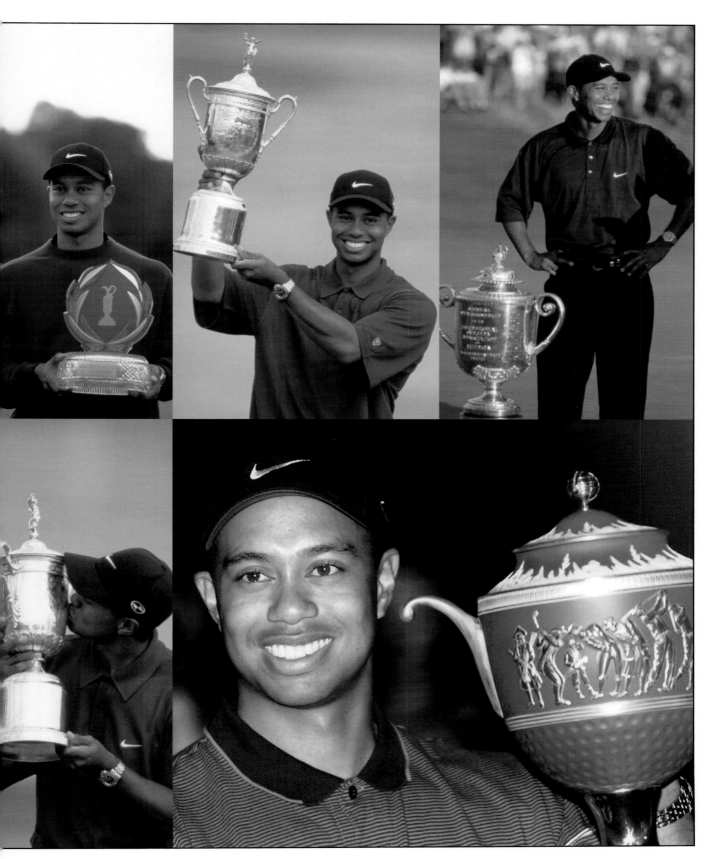

© Brian Spurlock (4); SIPA Press (1 - lower right)

PGA TOUR VICTORIES

2001

WGC-NEC Invitational

Bay Hill Invitational

The Players Championship

The Masters

The Memorial Tournament

2000

Mercedes Championship

AT&T Pebble Beach Pro-Am

Bay Hill Invitational

The Memorial Tournament

U.S. Open

British Open

PGA Championship

NEC Invitational

Bell Canadian Open

1999

Buick Invitational

The Memorial Tournament

Motorola Western Open

PGA Championship

NEC Invitational

National Car Rental/Disney

Tour Championship

American Express

Championship

1998

BellSouth Classic

1997

Mercedes Championship

The Masters

GTE Byron Nelson Classic

Motorola Western Open

1996

Las Vegas Invitational

Walt Disney Classic

PGA EUROPEAN TOUR VICTORIES

2001

Johnnie Walker Classic

Deutsche Bank Open

1999

Deutsche Bank SAP Open

2000

British Open

1998

Johnnie Walker Classic

U.S. AMATEUR VICTORIES

1994, 1995, 1996

U.S. Amateur Championship

1991, 1992, 1993

U.S. Junior Amateur Championship